Pisgah Press was established in 2011 to publish and promote works of quality offering original ideas and insight into the human condition, the realm of knowledge, and the world around us.

Copyright © 2021 Pisgah Press
Printed in the United States of America

Published by Pisgah Press, LLC
PO Box 9663, Asheville, NC 28815
www.pisgahpress.com

Story by Levi M. Plesset
Illustrations by Genevieve duCharme-Hill
Book & cover design: Iz Web, www.SocialConstruct.com

All rights reserved. No part of this publication may be reproduced, stored in a retrieval system, or transmitted, in any form or by any means, electronic, mechanical, photocopying, recording, or otherwise, without the prior written permission of Pisgah Press, except in the case of quotations in critical articles or reviews.

Library of Congress Cataloging-in-Publication Data
Plesset, Levi/Literally the Coolest Book

Library of Congress Control Number: 2021934737

Includes illustrations

ISBN-13: 978-1942016632

First Edition
First Printing
August 2021

This book is dedicated to Amelia Bedelia.

LITERALLY

THE COOLEST BOOK

written by Levi Plesset
illustrated by Genevieve duCharme-Hill

TABLE OF CONTENTS

Wild Goose Chase .. .. 2 & 3
Monkey Business.. .. .. .4 & 5
Out of This World.. .. .. .6 & 7
An Interesting Story behind You .. .. .8 & 9
Knock One's Socks Off .. .. .10 & 11
Put (Something) on the Map .. .. 12 & 13
Not One's Cup of Tea.. .. .. 14 & 15
Buried in Work.. .. .. 16 & 17
Wear a Lot of Hats.. .. .. 18 & 19
Get Cold Feet .. ..20 & 21
Be on the Fence.. .. .. 22 & 23
See Eye to Eye. .. ..24 & 25
Have a Ton of (Something) .. ..26 & 27

Explanations 29
A Note for Parents and Teachers. 30
More Idioms, Metaphors, and Similes. 31

INTRODUCTION

The word "literally" explains that the words you are using or reading mean exactly what they say—there's no double meaning, metaphor, or interpretation needed. For example, if your friend told you that it took her "literally forever" to read a book, that would mean she would be reading that book until the end of time!

But you may have heard the word "literally" used in a more modern context as an emphasis to a metaphor, which is its opposite meaning! Did you know that the word "thrift" originally meant prosperity rather than frugality? That, too, is its opposite meaning.

Language evolves just as people do. As we grow older, we learn more words and about word choice. It's really a wonderful thing that we can learn to express ourselves so personally and fully.

Lewis Carroll, in *Alice's Adventures in Wonderland*, wrote:

> "Then you should say what you mean," the March Hare went on.
>
> "I do," Alice hastily replied; "at least—at least I mean what I say—that's the same thing, you know."
>
> "Not the same thing a bit!" said the Hatter. "You might just as well say that 'I see what I eat' is the same thing as 'I eat what I see'!"

I hope this book engages you to think and learn about language. You are the master of your words! Enjoy them.

Pierre said, "Look, Julia, I'm inventing a time-travel machine!"

"Hah!" said Julia. "It sounds to me like you're on a wild goose chase."

WILD GOOSE CHASE

When Julia went to visit her family in the country, she **literally** went on a wild goose chase.

Mrs. Wachenschwon told the boys to cut out the monkey business when they were playing paper football in the classroom.

MONKEY BUSINESS

Capuchin monkeys have been trained as service animals for people who have suffered spinal cord injuries. This **literal** monkey business is a long-term job for these intelligent little primates.

Adrian thought his mother's homegrown heirloom tomatoes were out of this world.

OUT OF THIS WORLD

In 2019, NASA scientists peered farther into space than ever before to capture images of a celestial body that is **literally** out of this world.

Juan has an interesting story behind him—it's amazing to hear what he's done.

HAVING AN INTERESTING STORY BEHIND YOU

Juan **literally** has an interesting story behind him; in fact, his shelves are full of wonderful tales that he loves to read!

KNOCK YOUR SOCKS OFF!

Kamilia told Atiya that the newest book in their favorite series was going to knock her socks off.

The power surge from Atiya's experiments with electricity **literally** knocked her socks off.

Chuck Berry put rock and roll music on the map.

PUT SOMETHING ON THE MAP

When he sailed from Panama to Peru, Bishop Fray Tomas de Berlanga discovered the Galapagos Islands and **literally** put them on the map.

Jerome was worried about the race because building boxcars was not really his cup of tea.

(NOT) ONE'S CUP OF TEA!

Great-aunt Astrid had to remind Paul once again that the ginger and turmeric brewing in the pot were for her **literal** cup of tea.

TO BE BURIED IN...

As she got ready for her final exams, Jasmine was buried in homework.

Ancient Egyptians were **literally** buried in treasures that they would need in the afterlife.

Guadalupe wears a lot of hats: she directs movies, cooks wonderful meals, and is a community volunteer.

WEAR A LOT OF HATS

Guadalupe **literally** wears a lot of hats.

Andria got cold feet before her piano recital and resolved to practice more before she performed.

GETTING COLD FEET

Christian borrowed his father's goose-down booties to stay warm when he **literally** got cold feet.

ON THE FENCE

Luke was on the fence about what he should buy his sister for Hanukkah.

Luke was **literally** on the fence after retrieving his basketball from his neighbor's yard.

Tomas and Gina rarely see eye to eye about the rules when they play games together.

SEE EYE TO EYE

Patricia could hardly wait to be as tall as her twin brother Patrick— so they could **literally** see eye to eye.

Paige has a ton of friends in New York City.

Explanation of the Idioms

P. 2 — "A wild goose chase" can describe any activity that is futile.

P. 4 — "Monkey business" can refer to foolish behavior—or something you're not supposed to be doing!

P. 6 — "Out of this world" can describe something that's exceptional.

P. 8 — "An interesting story behind someone" (or something) can suggest that the person or object has an unusual, unexpected, or remarkable background.

P. 10 — "Knock one's socks off" can indicate that something is really impressive and awesome.

P. 12 — "To put something on the map" can refer to making something widely known or popular.

P. 14 — "My cup of tea" can describe something that you really like or do well—though it's mostly used negatively ("It's not my cup of tea").

P. 16 — "To be buried in" can mean completely immersed in a project, or overwhelmed by more work than you can handle.

P. 18 — "To wear a lot of hats" means a person has many diverse talents or does a variety of different things.

P. 20 — "To get cold feet" tells you that someone is so uncertain about a planned activity or course of action that they decide not to do it after all.

P. 22 — "On the fence" can be used to describe someone who is unsure about a decision.

P. 24 — "To see eye to eye" can describe people who are in agreement.

P. 26 — "A ton" is often used to convey a large, but nonspecific amount or number of something; it is actually a unit of measurement of 2,000 pounds.

A Note for Parents and Teachers

If the English language has a textbook, that book is the *Oxford English Dictionary* (or OED). The word "literally," according to the OED, means "in a literal, exact, or actual sense; not figuratively, allegorically, etc."

In 2011, the editors of the OED added that "literally" can be colloquially used "to indicate that some (frequently conventional) metaphorical or hyperbolical expression is to be taken in the strongest admissible sense: 'virtually, as good as.'" The update also says that the recently recognized definition is "now one of the most common uses, although often considered irregular in standard English since it reverses the original sense of literally ('not figuratively or metaphorically'). If "literally" is now an emphasis for metaphor, then we no longer have a word in the English language to distinguish the literal from the figurative. This book is a crusade to save the word "literally."

I wrote this book with the hope that parents encourage today's children to think about language and the words that they hear, speak, read, and write. Although this is a children's book, its intent is to serve as a tool for families to discuss the beauty, intelligence, and uniqueness of the English language. While some language lovers scorn the acceptance of the newer usages of "literally," I encourage young language learners to explore their own voice and lexicon, as the way in which one speaks is an identifier of one's individualism, personality, and world view.

Levi Plesset

Los Angeles, 2018

More Idioms, Metaphors, and Similes

Similes
As cold as ice
As cool as a cucumber
As deep as the ocean
As easy as pie
As fast as greased lightning
As free as a bird
As good as gold
As happy as a clam
As hot as a firecracker
As light as a feather
As neat as a pin
As old as the hills
As pretty as a picture
As slow as molasses (in January)
As smart as a whip
As smooth as silk
As strong as an ox
As sweet as honey
Like riding a bicycle
Like a ton of bricks

Verbal Metaphors
Add insult to injury
Beat around the bush
Bowled over by
Break a leg
Break the ice
Call it a day
Dodge a bullet
Feel blue
Judge a book by its cover
Let the cat out of the bag
Level the playing field
Reach for the stars
Reinvent the wheel
Rest on one's laurels
See the light
See the writing on the wall
Show them the door
Take it with a grain of salt
The tables have turned
Throw for a loop
Wear your heart on your sleeve

Noun Phrases
(an) Albatross around your neck
(a) Barrel of monkeys
(a) Bleeding heart
(a) Bone to pick with you
(the) Calm before the storm
(the) Elephant in the room
(a) Kangaroo court
(a) Piece of cake
(the) Pits
(a) Silver bullet

Other Idioms
At the drop of a hat
Barking up the wrong tree
Born yesterday
Cooking with gas
In on the ground floor
In a New York minute
In one's wheelhouse
Never met a stranger
On cloud nine
On the ball
Once in a blue moon
Out of left field
Over the moon
Over the top
Sink or swim
Thrown in the deep end
Tickled pink
To the ends of the earth
Under the weather
Underwater
Walking on air
Walking on thin ice
Working in a vacuum

_____

_____

www.ingramcontent.com/pod-product-compliance
Lightning Source LLC
Chambersburg PA
CBHW042354280426
43661CB00095B/1060